Anne Landers
Luminosity

Luminosity
ISBN 978 1 76041 846 5
Copyright © text Anne Landers 2020
Copyright © cover photo Erika Shankley – Tasman Island
Lighthouse at light-up time

First published 2020 by
Ginninderra Press
PO Box 3461 Port Adelaide 5015 Australia
www.ginninderrapress.com.au

Luminosity

Contents

Alter Ego	7
Opening	10
Papillon	11
The Mountain	12
Post-traumatic Stress	13
Communication	14
Fragments of Time	16
Pickled Things	17
The Feast	18
Tasman Island Revisited	23
Out of Time	25
It's Just Not Cricket!	26
The Multicoloured Scarf	28
Tumbling Over	29
Forgiveness	30
The Knitting Sister	31
Shipwreck	33
Regrets	35
Home Thoughts	36
Mother's Dreams	37
Hens in a Hole	38
Projections	39
Shooting Stars	40
Che	41
Grandad's Legacy	42
Outside	46
Murphy on the Road	47
Sparrow News	48
Four Eyes	49
Fantasy Froth	52
Wishes	53

Phone Calls	55
Eddystone Point Revisited	57
Bushfire	58
Welcome Stranger	59
The Empty Chair	61
Dog Wash	62
Springtime	63
Anniversary	64
Wheels of Life	66
Depression	67
Boxes	69
Adoption	71
InSanity	72
Conservation	73
Chocolate Confessions	75
The Dancers	77
Fred	78
Aftermath	81
Atavism	83
Cast the Net	84
Dialogue With a Doll	85
Cybernaut	87
Separation	88
Midwinter Blues	89
Mourning	90
Robbie	91
Time Warp	92
Walks	93
Whales	95
Behind the Screen	96
Celebration	98
Conflict	99
Let There Be Light	100

Alter Ego

Come in, my other self.
The door is opened wide
enough for us to reunite
and join
within a space
where fantasy and fact can coalesce –
and there within the void
create a living whole.
No more the need to fear
the hidden self
who brought survival
into the phantom world
where misery and deep despair
are mute offerings
on sacrificial altars
dark and drear.

With you I trod
on unknown earth.
I ventured deep
where even angels
sheltered in their wings.
At night or in the daylight hours
I craved your company
until from those who knew
the order came
'Abandon this – your dream must go!'
and so I bade farewell.
You cried then in despair
and fled my soul;
and I was left alone
in dark to weep,
'No more? No more
your blessed company keep?'

I seek again
this other self
a former part of me.
Hope rises with the gentle word
proclaiming destiny.
'Delight in this,
your inner child,
your creativity:
return once more to joy in life
and blessed normality.'
So heeding now
that whispered voice
I throw apart my psyche's arms
I welcome back
that inner self
that blessed part of me.

Opening

To the inner child lost through the years

You knock at the door of my heart in the night,
a tentative knock, because something's not right.
You whisper 'hello' with a scared little smile
and ask could you possibly stay for a while.
The door creaks and groans as it swings on its hinge
(It sounds just like you, when they tell you you whinge!)
But despite all the rust and the dirt jamming tight
you push at the door of my heart in the night;
and despite all my efforts to say my goodbyes
I am drawn to the door by the pain in your eyes.
And I just want to reach out and hold you again
and let you know that I'm feeling the pain
of a child, lost and lonely, unseen in a crowd
betrayed, violated, a waif in a shroud.
And I long now to hold you and hug you so tight
and let you know gently that everything's right
that the door has been oiled, the brass knob is clean
and the cage of the house of my heart is not seen.
So knock at the door of my heart in the night
with no fear or anguish, with no need for fight;
and I'll cherish and nourish with all of my might –
until you no longer need knock in the night.

Papillon

A farewell to Jesula Marius, my first international fosterchild in Haiti

My little butterfly
stretch your wings and rise to meet the sun.
Show your beauty
as you grow
and let the world see
your dignity and grace.
Through troubled times
and turmoil in your land
your love can shine,
just as the sun still shines
when hidden by the clouds.
And even though
you grow in height
and change,
you will always be
my little Papillon.

The Mountain

There is a mountain in my heart
it beckons me to come and walk
within the shadow of its hills
by bubbling stream and ferny stalk.

It beckons me to come and walk
along a memoried summer day
before the winter chills did throw
their frostbite on a child's play.

Within the shadow of its hills
we sang and danced the hours of youth.
With reckless joy we spent our days
forgetful we must face the truth.

By bubbling stream and ferny stalk
we met again in mountain chill
for we had grown and we could see
the past had gone, along with hill.

There is a mountain in my heart
with memories fond it calls to me
its sunshine and its winter rain
have washed away the grief and pain
I know we will not part.

(By bubbling stream and ferny stalk
within the shadow of its hills
it beckons me to come and walk.
There is a mountain in my heart.)

Post-traumatic Stress

So long ago it seems
I had my life
in my control
but now the slightest ask
the tiniest chore
can send me hurtling
through the space
within my brain
where secret things
lie buried
in the past.
My body has reacted
with a fury
of its own
demanding I repent
of tears not shed
or even
joys unlived.

Here in a place
where tongue and mouth
unite with brain
to ramble in the present,
past and future
combining three in one;
and helpless though I am
I found someone who
without condemnation
can help me make some sense
of what I write or do.

Communication

I sat in a train
outward bound from Warrnambool
and I heard people talking.
Of what were they talking?
Like a god, I sat and listened;
in my corner I sat and listened.
Their voices flowed around me
like sounds
at the sea-shore. And I listened.
I heard what they said
and what they didn't say.
I heard what they thought;
their love, their hate,
their unexcited expectancy of life;
of what they did, and what they wanted to do;
their fears, their thrills.
And no one, but I, heard.

I sat in a bar and listened,
and I heard the voice
of loneliness, anguish, despair.
Some were drunk and some were not;
but I heard their voices
and I wondered.
Where has humanity failed
that only in this place
could they speak?
Only when their minds were dulled
were they free
to reveal their desires and needs,
and reach out towards others.

I sat in the bush and listened
and I heard the sounds;
of wind in the trees,
the scuttle of mice
and a snake or two,
the little sounds that silence brings;
and far away,
with the muted roar of the surf,
I heard my own voice crying out;
for love
and warmth
and most of all
for the meeting of souls
that can only come with time.

But time stands still
unless we make the move to stretch out arms
and clasp the other outstretched hands.

Fragments of Time

So many fragments of self
scattered around my brain.
So many shards of life
piercing the here and now.
I pick up the pieces
one by one –
turning them over, assessing them,
filing them smooth
with insight
and communication.
The great silence breaking at last
piece by piece,
expelled into the air.

Some memories evaporate into the mists of time.
Others are chewed, digested and patched
into the reality of time and hindsight.
Scissor movements of electricity
jumping from cortex to memory banks,
providing its own solutions on the way.

The jigsaw starts to take form;
the picture emerges from the shadows,
each broken piece matched and fused
into an identity
called me.

The prism cracks, contorts,
the vacuum leaks and sound
can whisper forth.
The silence is broken.
I am heard.

Pickled Things

Pickled things
        that sit
                in jars
upon my pantry shelf
        have arms
and rings.

If they were
        in the sea
I'd be afraid.
        They're not
so I eat them.

The Feast

The Maiden waits in solitude

Within the shuttered room in state
awaiting her domestic fate
upon a marble floor.
With carved legs of cedar brown
and mirrored top in beeswax down,
the banquet table waits.
With table flaps in low retreat
and curtains closed to bar the heat
the silent chairs surround.
As summer now succeeds the spring
December too must usher in
the festive season fair.
Wailing cries of consternation
see the dust in crenellation –
prepare the way of cleaning.
Uneasy lie the myriad motes,
flotillas frenzied; churning boats
upon a wooden sea.
Dark retreats as windows open
doors ajar provide aeration
all unclean must leave.
Chattering cloths and humour bring
usher in on feathered wing
duster in its glory.
Roaring dragon follows after
sucking waste from floor and rafter
leaves unsullied sheen.

The maiden dresses

Pristine wood her clothes acquire
robe her in her white attire
starkness now bedecked.
Rosied wreaths will find no quarrel
with this maiden's festooned spoil
of the plundered farm.
Sacrificial piglet suckling
apple, lies by roasted duckling,
held asunder by the ham.
Potatoes roasted, white and orange
seem to pay the pumpkin homage
midst the greens of peas and beans.
Brazen breast of turkey flaunting
seasoned stew of giblets taunting
sweetmeats plattered taste.
Overflowing with the finery
sideboard's called to hold the winery
table's dress complete.

The feast commences

At the hostess's instigation
bell is rung for celebration
let the feast commence!
Throng to seat enraptured rears
oohs and ahs and many cheers
raise the lowest spirit.
Christmas candles conflagrate
as the feasters congregate
banquet must begin!

Lager flows enticing lather,
sparkling glasses raised to gather
compliments of flowing cheer.
Laughing sounds of expectation
usher in the celebration
birthday of a king.
Words of hope and songs of glory
tell again the age old story
timeless in a time-filled land.

The feast continues

Seating governed by the score
of who knows who, and human flaw,
involves some mediation.
Finally the seats are filled
(not always by the invite quilled)
excited voices babel.
Eyebrows raised in consternation,
glances chance interpretation,
not a maliced thought!
Scandal which appals a nation,
gossip in proliferation
bubbles with the wine.

Knife and fork with metal clatter
soon drowns out the loudest chatter
busy silence falls.
Hand to mouth in rapid flurry
finds and spears its latest quarry
feeds the grinding mill.
After all the vittles blending
(sweet delights seem never ending)
sated bodies slow.
Glazed eyes and slurry voices
minimise the need for choices
eating nearly done.
Slower now the forks are lifted
completeness with the hour drifted
somnolence required.
At last with food and wine replete
room with gossip is surfeit
drift away from table.

The maiden is left alone

Naked in her wantonness,
abandoned now by those she blessed,
broken lies the table.
Feast is finished, feast is gone
bridal dress is torn undone
shrouds replace tiaras.

Shutters close to block out heat
table flaps again retreat
doors are closed on covers neat
Christmas Day is over.

Tasman Island Revisited

Siren songs singing
in harmony humming,
whispering tales of silence and sea.
Crying a love song
for cliff and for island
calling, yes calling,
to all that I be.

Turn back the dream clock,
turn back to the mystery
of all that I am and
of all that I see.
Back in the yesteryear
from whence I have journeyed,
to Here-Now-Beyond
a completeness in me.

Yesterday's sorrow grows
through to tomorrow.
Tears in the winter
bring growth in the spring.
How sad when we fail
to live by that promise
of new birth and regrowth
that springtime will bring.

The song of the skylark
circuitous singing;
the rake of the rail as it clutters below;
the mutter of muttonbirds
mating and nesting
blends with the bark of the seal far below.

All these are sounds that
belong on my island
part of the being who carries away
all of the wonders, the sounds and the splendour
of Tasman who sits on her guard in the bay.

Out of Time

The clock struck one
and one again
then twice
and thrice
(That's three)

An hour more
the chime pealed four
plus two
by two
(make 4)

Through hours of night
it got things right
loud came the three and seven.
With ticking brain
(to make it plain)
add one to make eleven.

The witching hour
had passed by two
when shifting in momentum.
A quantum leap!
A loss of sleep!
An hour was lost forever.

Because, you see,
twixt two and three
the gears reversed their grinding.
And two times two
no more makes four
for daylight saving we're minding.

It's Just Not Cricket!

Christmas comes but once a year
and I say thanks for that
because as Christmas beckons me
with thoughts of fun and fancy free
long days of watching my TV –
the stumps of wood come out.

Christmas comes but once a year
and every time I see
Santa Claus repeat his role
of making 34th Street whole
or proving that he is a soul
before he is set free.

Christmas comes but once a year
I sigh in desperation.
The men in white come out to play,
they hit the ball and have their day,
the crowd in unison sing and sway,
I find no inspiration.

The Ashes come but once a year
and they roll back the cover.
But then they threaten a poor duck
that creature sure is out of luck
as from the air they seem to pluck
a maiden to bowl over.

The Ashes come but once a year
I think I know the reason.
For as they bat their legs turn square
their broken noses fill the air
and screwed up backs are not so rare.
Ah yes it's cricket season!

Christmas comes but once a year
I hope that's all forever
for as December trundles on
my leisure soon will be all gone
radio sings a sad swan song
and all I hear is whether.

Whether the Poms will bat or bowl
or if they'll take the wicket.
Whether the spin is fast or slow,
whether the crowd chants high or low,
whether they will ever know.
I think it's just not cricket!

The Multicoloured Scarf

In honour of my dear friend Pam, who knitted my scarf

Every day,
        hot or cold,
she wears the scarf.
Each stitch
a prayer
        for peace,
                healing,
                        love,
an end to pain.
Each bright band
        a rainbow
                of thoughts
slipping
        in and out
with the needles.
Each dark stripe
        a fear,
                a hurt,
                        a grief,
surrendered
and knitted
into the rosary
of the scarf.

Tumbling Over

Happy birthday, Sis!

You've climbed the stairs for many years
and now the paint is peeling;
the summit ever on before –
the past gone with it's dealings.
But now alas! you've reached the peak
it's time to tumble over
with grace and ease and ne'er a wheeze
into that field of clover.
Where old 'mares' rest amid the hay
and use their cunning wiles
to roll and play and go their way
with geriatric smiles.

You've found the Wrinkly gang – hooray –
a new life is beginning
10 years to Senior cards and cits,
and just 10 left for sinning.
Just 10 to practise charmed deceit
just 10 to drive in safety,
and then my dear you're in the sump
of baby boomer history.
But meanwhile – have a happy day
and think no more of trouble.
Just make the most of what it brings –
tomorrow may bring double!

Forgiveness

This raging river fills me;
savages my soul,
tears at my thoughts and dreams.
A torrent of insanity
sweeps the canyon of my consciousness
derelict of decent thought.

A desert of desolation
charging the jury to condemn
those responsible for this pain.
Judgements made within this moment
may take a lifetime to mend.

Yet all is not lost.

Deep within the desert
bubbles a spring
softening the harsh reality
of my hurt.
Tendrils of tenderness tug.
A riversong wild replete with love
wells up and forces through
the clay of clenched teeth.

Lips unwilling, open.
A shiver of silence;
A whisper of sound;
A breeze of gentle balm;
'I forgive'

The Knitting Sister

By dark of night when all do sleep
when dogs do howl and mice do creep,
while mortals rest in slumbers deep
she sits
and knits
alone.

As stitches drop and tempers rise
when purls and plains reach their demise
and hallway light shines in the eyes
she sits
and knits
alone.

When sitters knit and knitters sit
when all the lights in house are lit
it's time to say goodnight and quit
the knitting
sitting
sister.

Knitting needles all suspending,
great production now impending,
time and effort seem unending.
Click the needles in and out
slowly surely without doubt
grows the Herculanean beanie.

With the dawn the needles jaded
sense the night-time peace invaded
crawl away to dreams unfaded;
still upon the needles grey
rows of knit in strict array
slumber through the daylight hours.

Shipwreck

The ship went down
and all were saved,
the life raft launched and all aboard
uninjured though
adrift at sea
no comfort but companion hope
to ease the long cold days.
Then with the dawn of each new day
no rescue ship to bring relief.
Drifting, drifting, land in sight,
even lighthouse in the night
but never seen from shore.

Sustained by thoughts
of landlocked life
they drifted with the tides,
until a wilful eddy threw
their craft upon the sand.
Hope rose again, but quickly crushed
by walls of teatree, scrub and rock,
there seemed to be no hope.

Again there rose the vestige strength
of three determined men.
Battle ranks formed to force retreat
of valley, hill and bushland wild;
mindset focused, do or die,
sustaining every hard-fought step
until a track was reached.

A miracle must surely be;
a hum of tyres,
a gravelled screech,
appeared a truck
in logging road.
The shipwrecked crew were found

And valiant struggles
fought and won
found road and traffic –
A truck
a driver
and safety.

Seven men from ten returned.
Over hundreds of miles
they fought the sea,
they conquered the land,
and with unquenchable spirit
they survived.

Regrets

You curled up in the space
between two tree roots,
tired and sleepy,
driven from your hole by rain,
and you didn't care if I saw you.
You lay
tired and sleepy and lethargic,
but I have intelligence
and I know
in another month you would defend
with utter venom
your life. You would strike
with poison fangs
and no redress on either side.
So, with my higher intelligence,
I took advantage
of your hibernation.
I took a stick and hit you.
And not content with that
I returned with a better stick
and I hunted you –
so tired and sleepy
and I killed you
and then I proudly proclaimed my victory.
I measured your length
and said what damage you might have done.
A copperhead snake,
so dangerous to man,
so beautiful in your own territory.

Home Thoughts

A toadstool is a happy home although the lights are dim
to turn them up would cook a meal fit for any king.
A mansion on a hill so high has views both far and wide;
but vacuuming of all those rooms a chore I could not bide.
A log house in the bush out there appeals a lot to me
but then I think of all those draughts and know it cannot be.
A high-rise apartment way up north might satisfy my needs
but how would I be occupied without the garden weeds?
So try a fancy tree-house then way out in forest deep
but after weeks of squat and sit we'd be removed by creeps.
A flat might suit my lifestyle more now that I'm of age,
but would the dog content herself if found in such a cage?
The neighbours trees o'erhang the fence; their roots invade my lane
their leaves defy the borderline and soak up all the rain.
So near the shops I still can walk. No scooter, car, or cart
are needed here, just two old legs and stick on slippery path.
As old age comes I think much more of comfort, warmth and ease
so staying in my small abode will fulfil all my needs.

Mother's Dreams

My mother dreamed of far off towns.
Her dreams were woven through
a life of toil and need and want,
her dreams were strong and true.

My mother dreamed of countries far.
When hills were steep and long
her chariot tales would bear us up
transforming cries to song.

My mother dreamed of children fair
to laugh and play and rest
and even though the dream was broken
her life was filled with zest.

My mother dreamed of worldly flight
of journeys far and wide
and when her three score years arrived
her dreams rode with the tide.

Hens in a Hole

Three little hens in the garden today
scratch at my feet as I break the clay
fill in the hole where a plant should stay
and happily scratch it out.

Strong clawed feet to flatten the ground:
beak to peck at the slugs around:
red eye focused on what I have found
pecking to try it out.

Soft throaty questions tell me they're near
just in case my vision ain't clear
and even the dog they do not fear –
one pecks her on the snout!

I like to dig with my girls at my feet:
they all come running my voice to greet
flapping and squawking their food to meet
and table manners to flout.

Projections

Who will lift me from my bed
when I am dead?
Will they put me in my box
without my sox?
In view of my veracity
remembering my sagacity
will they think of me pragmatically
when I am dead?

Or will they wonder of the fun
when I am done?
Will they look at stars in darkened sky
with tearless eye?
Recalling my capacity
for loving with tenacity
will they sigh pathetically
when I am gone?

I like to think you'll cry for me
when dead I be.
I like to think that flowers will bloom
upon my tomb.
Without undue morosity
and no less animosity
I like to think you'll pray for me
when dead I be.

Shooting Stars

Last night
from my window
I saw some shooting stars but
they were not stars
that stay in the sky.
Instead they hurtled down
in streaks of gold and white
       lingering in my eye
dissolving into darkness.
A brilliant end to a sad life
or
was it a sad end
to a brilliant life?

Che

Died July 2018

There was a little cat
who took a little nap
right in the middle of the doorway.
When she was thin
it wasn't such a sin
but now she is fat, she fills the hallway.
If you look her in the eyes
she stares back in surprise
'But I am only doing what we felines do!
Take one step upon my tail
and I'll let out such a wail
then the RSPCA will apprehend you.
If you think you own the place
hang your head in such disgrace
it's obvious to me who runs the joint here.
Just step widely right around –
I'll not make a single sound
for my claws were invented to cause fear.
So learn from those before
do not try to use the door
else havoc and my wrath will rake upon you.
Feed my dinner right on time;
be quick to toe the line;
and we'll get along without you feeling blue.
So now the rules are bare
and you're tearing out your hair
I will go and rest upon the sofa;
I've changed my mind you see
and forever it will be
that I'm the cat and you're the lowly go-for.'

Grandad's Legacy

I wander now around my garden bed
and count the plants within which bear your mark.
How precious the memories they tell
of times we spent
and fortunes ploughed and shared.

Here in the lane Agonis curls its leaves
and stretching, branches reach to touch the earth.
Each convoluted leaf curl nestles close
and drooping, weeps in silhouette the shape.
(The times we spent on ladders pruning yours!
Impossible heights on tottering ladders reached,
held in safety by your hands)

'What grace!' the neighbours cry in passing by my gate.
'Magnificence! Where can I buy this plant?'
And when they venture deep into my lane
'What an awesome plant' they cry again.
'Where did you find this long-lost symbol of the past?'
and I reply, 'It came from Grandad's place.'
Yours are the fiercesome bromeliads
which bite the hand that feed it on the way.
(Ah yes. The hours we spent in planting patterned shades
from caravan to path;
the driftwood carried twice from here to there
and back again,
where now within my yard it grows them once again).

And yours the tall, thick Philomena flowers
behind the aviary, their awesome heads of layered
pink amid the dark, dark leaves.
(We shared together in the pain
of friends who passed before.)
Our Robby and our Ben lie
within your garden there;
they rest beside the caravan
in sweet tranquillity
while Laddie lies beneath the lawn
to greet the morning sun.

Around the corner here
a Clivea lurks in shade,
near Arum lily,
velvet and resplendent
in its purple shades, near black,
which turn in sunlight to a richer deeper hue.

Reposing 'neath the Margaret Davis tree of
pinks and whites are nearby serpentry
of snake's head lilies
peering from their dappled symmetry.
(With each small ant or snail you taught ability
to live with nature's gifts in harmony –
for each there is a task which is a part
of life – except for mosquito sting which wages war
upon your person, so beware!)

Within my porch a Hoya winds its way
and weeps its coral nectar tears on epiphytes below,
Haemanthus spreads its ears with luscious green
to warm within the rays of sun
each metre leaf of lengthy thickness seen.
(What hours we spent beneath the lemon tree
creating a bed of these!)

Veldthania sends its bell like flowers forth
to herald the arrival of the tri-shaped seeds
each one to sprout in robust fecundity
a new desired plant.
And there within the shelter of my door
The Crucifix Orchid sprouting more and more.

Each spade of mulch I set upon my plants
reminds me of the hours upon your roof
abucketing the spouts and casting to the ground below
a mixture rich and rare.
And with each raindrop on my head
I laugh aloud and think of times
when each first flurry of drops upon your head sent you below
to leave me (unrelenting) in the rain.
Each turn within my garden reflects of thee
a dazzling range of plants and parquetry.

We mixed together you and I
a chaos of colour and versatility.
Yours the clipped precision of the yew
and mine the careless scattering of pine
and rose and annual levity.
Who would have thought that such ambiguity
could shape together a collage of same plants
and produce such tranquil equanimity?

I cannot miss you when you leave this coil
for in my garden you bequeath your toil.

Outside

Outside my window trees sway and bend
dipping and swinging in tune with the wind.
Spring blossom showers
of petals and flowers
blow past my window in stormy delight.

Outside my window the clouds scud and hurry,
churning and milling like sheep in a pen.
Cold springtime showers
hit gardens and bowers
urging the daffodils into new life.

Outside my window the morning has broken,
sunshine is calling to shorten the night.
Early rays searching
for buds that are bursting,
filling my garden with warmth and with light.

Outside my window folk wander by slowly,
stopping to wave or to chat or just smile.
No need for a reason
to soak up the season –
just revel in springtime's mischievous wiles.

Murphy on the Road

a hair-raising ride in a motor car

'Jist look at that idiot up in front.
Jist look at the way he drives.
If it weren't for sensible folk like me
There'd be nobody left alive!'

'Tut tut,' said the off side passenger man,
'Tut, tut' from the back seat too.
'Sure Hell would freeze over and Heaven as well
if it weren't for drivers like you!'

'Jist look at the wimmin' around on the road,
why they not kilt I dunno.
The worse thing they did was give them the vote.
Since then it's been blow after blow.'

'Tut, tut,' said the front seat, shutting his eyes.
'Tut, tut,' from the rear as well.
'Fer God's sake, Murphy, watch the road
or we'll all end up in Hell.'

'And then of course there's the Ls and the Ps,'
(unperturbed as he ran a red light).
'If they all stayed at home and kept right out of cars
we'd start to get something right.'

'Oh no,' said the front seat, as white as chalk,
'Dear God.' cried the back seat again.
'Just let us out, there's no room on the road
For a driver all mouth and no brain.'

Sparrow News

Tumbling, hustling
chittering
like a flock of sparrows.
The door bursts open
again
and bodies fall through
a-scatter.
Feet pounding, thumping,
running
down to the phone-box
again.
Sunday morning
7 a.m.
(no Mass today – too excited)
Disembodied voice,
hollow with distance,
amused,
exasperated,
busy,
'Is it born yet?'
but this time
there's news.
'Yes yes yes!
You have a sister!'
Loud hoorays through street
(remember it's Sunday)
telling everybody.
Asleep?
Wake up!
Share the joy.
She's BORN.

Four Eyes

I woke up this morning
and what did I see?
I looked in the mirror
but I couldn't see ME!

                    I looked for my sneakers
                    and I looked for my sox
                    I looked for my tank top
                    and I looked for my box

I looked for my jumper
And I looked for my vest.
I wanted my teacher
to see me the best.

                    I was like an orange
                    who's skin has gone furry
                    I wanted to see
                    but my eyes were all blurry.

Then I got scared
and started to cry
Mummy came in
and asked me why.

                    But when I told her
                    she began to giggle
                    'Oh dear oh dear, Cameron
                    You are in a pickle!'

You can't find your shoes
or your socks or your vest.
Not even your face
To look at your best.

                Remember last night
                when I tucked you in bed?
                Remember what went
                on the stand near your head?

I thought long and hard
and I thought inside out
and all of a sudden
I gave a great shout.

                I felt with my hand
                at the side of the bed
                and I found my spare eyes
                where I'd put them instead.

I slipped on my glasses
with care, lest they broke
and all of a sudden
it was like I'd just woke!

                So I found my vest
                and my sneakers and sox
                and I found my shirt
                and my moth in a box.

I found my breakfast
and I found my school bag,
I brushed my hair so
I did not look a dag.

> I woke up this morning
> And what did I see?
> I looked in the mirror
> AND I COULD SEE ME!

Fantasy Froth

Fields of froth flow
in laced drapery.
Diamante glitters
adorn this bridal train,
rising and falling
with each body breath.
Colours of the rainbow
in
minuscule bubble mirrors,
reflect a thousand flames
nodding and dancing,
while the shadows
leap and stretch
upon the walls
of imagination and plaster.

But ah!
Too soon this bath grows cold
and I must return
from this fairy-tale wedding
with the bubble bath
to find my handsome prince
among the living.

Wishes

Thank you for asking

Just for once
I wish I could say how bad the pain
without your eyes shutting me out.
Just for once
I wish I could say
how really bad I feel
without you saying
'That's good'
and wandering off to more rewarding targets.

Just for once
behind the smile
I wish you heard me cry a while
I really wish you took the time
to listen and to feel.

I wish you cared
how bad the pain,
how much I long for
genuine care.
I wish I wasn't
just a whimpering
burden.

Despite the fact
I make a joke
and take the blame
and take a poke
at my stupidity
I wish…

Because you know
if I were aware
that you were there
to really care
then I could clear the terror from my mind.

I wish for once that you would hear
my horror and my deepest fear.
I wish in fact that you would sense
beyond bravado and defence.

I wish
you would
really
listen.

Phone Calls

Another phone call
another night.
In the weariness of the morning hours,
while the world sleeps
unaware of mortal turmoil,
incessant tones
demand my presence.
Sometimes
when I answer
the silence intones despair,
or
imagination flies
on panicked wings
of paranoia;
and visions
promising safety,
security
and solace
surely lie
at this end of the line.
I listen
as
the wires
shriek accusation
abuse
and sweating fears
why
        why
                why?

The grindstone of insanity
perceiving visioned wrongs
demand my heart and soul
until
torn apart
I crumble
and acquiesce.

Eddystone Point Revisited

Here is the essence of time unfurled –
a monumental moment of my life –
and not a trace to show.
No mark on the wall
no odd sock left behind.
I've been erased
by 20 years of disoccupation,
the only reminder
the snake at the entrance gate
that still eludes his captors
writing his own history book.

And yet –
the house is not unfriendly,
as if the stones have
searched their granitine crystal
and found an atom of familiarity,
a cosmic particle of history
that knew me by name
and measured me
against an infinity of time.
A mote of maternity
that stretched its arms and whispered
'Welcome home.'

Bushfire

Farmer! Seek around your paddocks, search the bush and river flats.
Not a place escaped this fury, this mad demented holocaust.
Whipped to fury by the north wind, smoking embers sprang to flame;
tinder grass and eucalypt exploded, throwing flaming tongues.
Now you search your once fine farmland, search your wasted, blackened hills,
hope perchance to find some cattle huddled in a sheltered rill.
Animals roasted in their pastures mutely, dumbly plead for death;
trusting eyes on man, their saviour, know the bullet means relief.
God in Heaven! Look upon him in the midst of Hell on earth;
send him rain to hide the starkness and the blackening, sickening death.

Welcome Stranger

Congrats! I cry.
You live in a waterproof house,
possibly you own it.
You have
       breakfast
               lunch
                       and dinner
if you want it.
You drink water from a tap
and it doesn't make you ill,
or even kill you.
If you get cold you put more clothes on.
If you get hot
you take them off.
That is your right of course
you've earned that
simply by being born here
and living in peace with no conflict.
It's tough – you can feel sorry for them,
those others who certainly have not earned those rights
probably never done anything to deserve it.
They certainly should never expect to come here
and deny us of our rights
which of course they will.

After all what do they expect
Shelter?
       Welcome?
               Safety?

We are proudly Australian
and welcome the right people to our shores –
A caring country
where we respect and love all others
as long as they are
                the right colour,
                          shape,
                                      wear the right clothes
and speak fluent English.
Prejudiced?
Are you kidding?
No way, mate!
Just blind,
        ignorant
                and biased.
True Australians.

The Empty Chair

It's not the right car at the end of the drive
and it's not the right person limping up it.
It's not the right dog in the car in the drive
and the coffee cup sits empty waiting.
The kettle runs dry as it whistles and sighs
the biscuits lie still in the barrel
and of all the herbs in my cupboard and store
there is no one there to explain them.
There is no one there to explain the pain
of a friend that was suddenly taken;
just a tear in my eye as I try to say why
my heart feels as though it is breaking.
We bantered and fought,
we quibbled and sought
to find common ground for our sparring,
but when all's said and done
we discovered the fun
of the friendship which we were making.

Dog Wash

Cute little bottom
tidied and neat.
Shaggy hairs banished
down to the feet.
Nails clipped, short now
mouth clean, breath sweet,
now you can't scratch me
each time we meet.
Pink bow necklace
adds to the charm
makes you an angel
without any qualm.
Smelling of roses
aroma so pure,
out of the dog wash
and in my front door.

Springtime

In the darkest chill of winter, when the days are long and cold,
when everything is gloomy and the world seems put on hold,
then I sit by my window and watch the raindrops fall
and wonder if these dismal days will ever end at all.
But one day as I scurry to the shops, in wind and rain,
I see a golden daffodil nod at me in the lane.
Then, as if my eyes are opened, all around me I can see
the little signs that nature gives when she sets earth free.
The tiny buds with blossom sprigs their autumn fruit bequeath;
The maple twigs in silhouette now breaking into leaf;
The bees buzz round with stores of gold, their liquid sun to make
and birds wing in from distant shores to nest there by the lake.
In an enervating uplift of the spirit I can see
that the favourite time of all the year is springtime – just for me.

Anniversary

I need to talk
about what Woodsie said
I call him Woodsie because he was my friend;
he must have been, to know me oh so well.
He knew I was unfit
to rear a son.
So very wise was he
he knew it all
he knew so many things.

Today I hung the curtains in my home.
They didn't fit
they didn't fit at all.
Projected in the room a sterile curse
unable to convey
my love, my warmth
my aching, bleeding heart.
I cursed the wrappings hung
around my panes
and cried despair.

How could he know
in twenty minutes short
the bond between my children?
The love between a mother and a son?
The tie connecting
these two infant minds?

Today I contemplate
what might have been
if you had stayed with me.
Visions of hope and trust
flowing in a descendant stream
of grandchildren
towards the future.

What is her name?
Does she cry
or does she peaceful lie
unknowing of the need for ancestry

Wheels of Life

So many wheels in front
so many roads behind.
I've travelled the many paths of life
a child, an adult, a mother, a wife.

The child rode a bike or trike
– 2 wheels, 3 wheels who cares what;
invented her games –
controlled her own destiny –
alone in her perfect world.

The adult grew away from visions –
drove full speed into reality.
Life not always kind –
collisions with brutality.

Then four sweet wheels rolled into play.
A bundle held in softened arms,
mewling much as kittens do,
prammed in autumn sunshine
driving maternal instincts
to guard and treasure.

So life rolled on!
And now each week
with 4 strong wheels
I journey up and down the lawn
engine crying 'I'm in charge'
truncating every varied blade
exorcising demons of the shade
and planning this year's journey.

Depression

Somewhere I have lost my way
the grey horizon weighs me down,
the cyclone storm from deep within
leaves me lost to laugh or sing.
Tumult deep within my soul.
Hurricane-hurling arrows speed
their way, to where my thoughts
and psyche panic-stricken lie.
To move with joy,
to dance in sheer delight of life
has been my fairytale wish
for eons of eternity.
To cry again for happiness or fold
into a belly-laugh
is but a dream.
The typhoon Anger rages surreality
deep, deep below this island rock and cage
within the mask of what I seem to be.

But you my friend, my love, my joy,
you know and sense it all;
the times of dark and futile fear,
the pain within,
the cold and hungry yearning for your love
so freely given, so often spurned and offered yet again.

Your silken greyness is the better kind
wrapping in warmth and generous touch.
It fills the aching void and
quiets the desperation
of my cry
with engine sounds of noise
and ectoplasmic touches on my soul.
And when my spirit quiets once again you
wrap your paw so gently on my breast
and there we sleep
together
through the night.

Boxes

Gelignite boxes there by the score,
apple cases, palings, and anything more
became in a twinkle
yachts, ships and planes,
cars, motorcycles
and fast racing lanes.

You were the captain
if I was first mate.
Sometimes came mutiny
sooner than late.
Who would have guessed that
of such simple means
came such imaginings,
came such dreams.

Such built my childhood
so passed my youth,
anything made of wood
turned to good use;
and if they were needed
for groceries buy,
cardboard though clumsy
replaced the supply.

The worst time for us, though
was winter's dark chill,
when seaworthy models
for flames were a fill.
As cold winter weather
chilled through to the bone
consigned to the fire
our vessels were gone.

Then broken-hearted
with paper and pen,
next seasons creations
took on a new form.
Resigned to necessity
we spent winter days
planning adventures
and summer dreams haze.

Adoption

We walked into the room, in the hospital,
trembling, afraid.
How could we turn you away
even if we didn't like you?
Then you came in
carried in the arms of someone who cared
and we just sat and stared,
too frightened to touch you
yet longing to cuddle and protect you.

She left us to dress you,
to change your nappy; to put on the finest dress –
quite impractical of course –
all those buttons…so she suggested a nightie,
and with a fistful of thumbs even that was difficult.
But we covered it with a shawl
and drove to a quiet place just to gaze at you
our baby!

You cried and cried, and all our love
couldn't cover your upset at the uprooting.
But by and by we convinced you
that we loved you.
Your mother receded in memory until but a vague shadow
remained of her; then that faded too.

But will the memory ever fade for her?
She loved you enough to bear you.
Love her. Respect her. She made
the greatest sacrifice woman can make.
She gave you into unknown hands trusting
implicitly in their love.

InSanity

So here again
you knock at my door,
ringing my bell in the midst of the night,
saying we owe it to set things aright,
screaming your anguish with all of your might,
until we lie battered and bent.

Nobody wonders if we can survive
nobody wants to hear.
Nobody knows of the terror we've seen
nobody cares where our family has been
nobody wants to be in between
a mad woman and her fears.

Paranoia happens in books,
not in reality,
not in the home.
Genius intellect happens to know,
warped intelligence sharpens the blow,
shafts of venom with accuracy throw
into the depths of my soul.

Christ on the mountain
did think of these
the least of his brethren.
Blessed the mournful for though they shall weep
blessed indeed are the folk that they keep
and blessed the harvest they reap.
Blessed the meek for they shall survive
blessed the humble their spirits revive
blessed the crazy they'll not be deprived
while charity bleeds in the hall.

Conservation

A world without 'roo?
Must this my children see?
Live in a land bereft of wild things;
no song of joy from birds, or cry
of the hunt from devil
on the run.
How will we feel
when breakers stop their roll,
and stars
no longer glimmer in the sky?
Will we rejoice?
Will humans shout their glee
from barren hill
at lightless world
where sun no longer shines?

Our children walk the bush, the silent bush.
No thump as wallaby takes alarm,
no laughing song
of kookaburra, high in tree,
no lizard rustle in the dead dead grass.

Leave them this world
though animals few there be;
though hillsides slide on treeless roots
to fill the valleys below
and sugar gliders wing
forever to the unknown landing place.
Let us fight for what remains, and hope
our children have more sense
and wonderment than we,
and life will return to the ravished land
gradually.

Chocolate Confessions

On the inside looking out
I find I must proclaim my doubt.
Why with your addictions 'fessing
should you get a chocolate blessing?
Heretic I well may be
but you in spirit cannot see
that molten chocolate at it's best
will surely lead you to distress.
From the outside looking in
I warn you now with teary hymn
that this brown liquid so will dare
your taste buds and your soul ensnare,
calling with seductive flavour
whilst promising a lifetime favour.

(Oh surely such a heretic
in inquisitions finer pick
shall burn at stake and surely take
the recipe for highest bake
in blessed twigs and flame so high
that her own words shall prove a lie.)

Well, now I pledge your yearning heal
no longer warm brown eats reveal.
You will in future not respond
to lust and love of liquid blond
nor indeed of temptress brown
of any shape, or taste to down.
And though I seek to bring you peace,
I fear that craving will not cease –
those chocolate beans, I hear, inspire
sensuous taste and celestial fire.
Unable to defeat the whim
I foresee a future dim
where addiction gravely felt
leaves you limp and poorly dealt.
While I, a freedom loving creature
shall be led to gentle laughter.

The Dancers

I watched them dance
        into the air
        of adulthood
and in despair
I asked them then
        if they would stay,
I could protect them
keep them safe…
'But no' they answered,
strong of voice,
the future beckons
        dancing feet.
I let them go,
        I let them see
tomorrow days
        forgetting me.
I let them dance
        the world to greet.
And now alone
        until we meet
        I sit and wait
                for dancing feet.

Fred

a dog of distinction in the town of Penguin

Our Fred he was an honest chap
a man of high degree
where'ere he went he left a trail
a doggie trail of pee.
The ladies swooned as he went by
their canine hearts were full
This Casanova broke their hearts
but still they felt his pull.
His satin smooth and svelte suit
of black and white were pure
the lady dogs were drawn to him
as with magnetic lure.
Their limbs they did capitulate
As honest Fred walked by –
the weakness of the muscle tone
just could not tell a lie.
Such handsome mate had not been seen
for many, many years
and as he strode, our Freddie's mode
brought forth the ladies' tears.
With loves dear grin they laid them down
his favour hoping find
but as he careless passed them by
lovelorn were they in mind.

Our Fred was very debonair
He knew he was top dog.
No need to fight, no time to play
just endlessly to jog.
Our Fred he ran on 4 strong legs
upon the beach and path.
He climbed the gate, he roamed the street,
he ran through fence and grass.
Yet never did his darting form
deny a moment low;
this Casanova of the world
assigned from Cupid's bow.
A wilful dog – a sprightly man
the white tail jigged and bobbed
betraying where he ran and hid
to his annoyance dobbed.
But Fred's love dance was just a show
No little Freds to see
The bitches they swore chastity
Fred's day was not to be.

Our town will be a little less
now Fred has left the race.
Will take a mighty terrier
to ever fill the space.
Though now long gone, our Fred will roam
forever on our shore –
a wraith of all the history
that makes up canine lore.

Vale, Fred.

Aftermath

Wander now, through blackened forest;
rest awhile, by haunted stream
overfilled with darkest memories
man can no more dare to dream.
Come and visit once – gay household
where we sat on summer's night
breathing in the balmy gum – smell,
wondering at the possum's flight.
Come! Sit down within my ashes;
hang your coat upon the ground
and gaze upon the desolation
that stretches mile on mile around.

What could we do with this fury
this unleashed monster, flaming, wild,
searing all it caught and plundered,
Pirate Fear and Horror's child?

Mile on mile of crumbling chimneys
mutely pleading with the sky,
starkly staring at the hillside
and the scorched trees that die.
Yellowing leaves that quickly wither
sighing softly, flutter by,
gather in their mourning thousands,
flutter, rustle there they lie.

Numb and dazed and shot with anguish
we stand by our smouldering home
blankly stare at ashen ruins,
thoughts to come will fill a tome.

But the grey clouds slowly gather
blotting out relentless blue,
damping down the smoke and fires
helping us to start anew.
For nature soon responds to rain clouds;
gathers strength and pushes through
filmy veil of gossamer greenery
in gullies and on hillsides too.
And in the fields the stricken cattle
grateful, sigh and softly low;
find new strength and find new scenery
as their fodder starts to grow.

And with the veil of greenery spreading,
softening deepest sharpest blow
courages flickers, wakes and quickens
seeds of Hope and Future sow.

Atavism

Elation – rifle in hand
who sees who – the hunter or hunted?
Equal chance.
For one the chance to crouch and hide
or run and leap
too fast for the eye to follow
let alone the bullet.
For the other – the peace of the walk,
the breeze in your face;
and keen anticipation of the kill.
The hunter still exists:
no denying the thrill of the hunt!
and yet
you and I sit here in harmony.
I eat my tea, and feed you
your meal of carrot and parsley
and find you don't like radish or apple!
Between us is mutual respect.
I feed you, or you die
for you are caged – because you are so young
and unprotected.
But soon your instinct will take over.
Fear will replace respect and I will release
and cease to love.
You will be the hunted
and I the hunter.
The cycle begins again.

Cast the Net

People fish on ebbing tides
of traffic sounds.
Surging currents far and wide
of horns and bells;
long line flung to reel in
metal monstered trams;
island safety nets
a haven for the busy
or the brave.
If time and space were measured here
then surely coalesced
within its frame
one lonely man
last seen in Swanston Sstreet
would vanish in the swell.

Dialogue With a Doll

We are older now, you and I.
Do you know your wig is falling off?
My hair isn't falling off, it's just thinner.
Companion of my childhood,
uncomplaining advocate
my friend.
You show me once again
the need to cry.
You take me back to the innocence
of childhood,
you fill me again with the magic
of moments at night
where, under the blankets,
released from the day's miseries
I shared your china and bisque company.
You and I,
sharing the day, joy and sorrow,
love and hate, good and bad.
We found rainbows
and sunshine
and bright green meadows
where we could run and jump
and play together
until, worn out,
we fell asleep
side by side.

Tonight you fulfil that dream again.
You take away my fear,
and draw me back to Then
but keep me Now
when I wander too far
in memory and become
bogged in the mire
that life seems to bring.

Sometimes I wonder
how I ever thought you were cuddly
with your jointed limbs
and china smile.
But I never wonder
that the friendship between
a child and a doll
can last through generations.

Cybernaut

This space between my ears is filled
with cybernetic junk
no more will I be energised
by your average street type punk.
I now get lost in outer space
and not a Melways map;
road rage cannot be exercised
you cannot hear the c—p!
The shifting vision of the Web
must satisfy my needs;
intrepid exploration there
results in mighty deeds.
Yet still I strive and still I fail
to find the download knob
so two flat feet and trusty car
will prove the better mod.

Separation

The house grows cold.
No creaking board beneath the foot;
no warmth upon the lounge or seat
an icy chill around the heart.
This pain will never go away –
so terrible this aching beat.
My other half is severed now
and lies alone in deathly chill.

It's raining now upon my cheeks
an Arctic blast of winter ice,
a shriek of anguish keening round;
for I must stay whilst you are gone.
Within the lonely chapel light –
within the box that holds his shape
he lies in wait – eternally.

The morrow brings a long farewell
the public face of private grief.
Tonight our spirits kiss goodbye
as homeward bound you fly.

Midwinter Blues

Sullen sea surging, sweeping and soaking
spewing up spoils sucked up from the shelf.
Birds swooping, soaring, salaciously scavenge
the debris, thrown up by a spindrifted sea.
Whining and whirling, grasping and groaning
wind plucks the living and quickly moves on,
capricious, uncaring, destroys in its pathway,
wrecks and recovers and whirls ever on.
Whipped into fury the sea beats at doorstep
of time and dominion, home and retreat.
Leaves on the sea sands little brown platypus
broken and soft, fragility bent.

Not so different this spume driven fury
shaking the earth and the air with its strength.
Thoughts tumble down in tumultuous tendrils
twisting and turning along with sea's length.
In the surge and the wallow of emotions unsweet,
action frenetic, tasting defeat,
there in my tempest, distracted and bruised,
comes a sweet lightness of words never used.

Now the waves mellow, retreat and diminish;
calmer and quiet in tune with the breeze.
Seas slow and slacken, froth to the foreshore
leave but a trace of the elements squeeze.
Calmer and quiet so too are the visions
sweeter the memories of years gone before.
Emotions congealing,
thoughts are revealing
froth of before-life now left on the shore.

Mourning

Death came stalking in the tiny town.
Stunned into awakening
before the battering blow,
for one brief moment,
the men knew their assailant
but slid into the ever-reaching
darkness of the night –
as did their murderer.

Death came gently in the tiny town.
Touched into sleeping
by loving hands,
the pain of years
washed away with gentle tears,
easing the steps
into the lasting light –
but the mourners remained.

Robbie

A song for our miniature Scotch Collie sadly missed

Run through the hills and the meadows,
run through the grassy glen,
run over mountains and valleys
till you come home again.

Run with the breezes blowing;
run with the wind and the rain,
run, ever smiling and laughing
till you come home again.

Up where the clouds are chasing
sheep herded high in the sky,
forever young, free and happy,
on the rainbow bridge you'll fly.

We'll miss your song in the morning;
we'll miss your bark at the gate,
but when the shadows go flying
at Heaven's door you will wait.

Run faithful friend, through the meadow,
run bristlehound through the glen,
run, till the bagpipes sighing
welcome you home again.
Run, Robbie, run.

Time Warp

Into the next generation I tumble
flip flop.
Eager questions
hazy answers,
searching the years
for things beyond recall.
The arrogance of youth gone,
the certainty of memory
no longer safe.
Places, events swirling together
into a timeless warp.
The only consolation is that
all my friends have fallen
into this time warp
too.
I've become the next
teller of tales –
the bearer of past events
of oral history
on a minute scale.
I've searched the wilderness
of bygone years
for the episodes that marked my life
and found satisfaction
in their incompleteness.

Walks

Walk this way the child said
tugging at my sleeve
my treasures all
are in the hall
so come this way with me.

Walk this way the teacher said
and hold your head up high
at work be neat
and never cheat
and troubles will be shy.

Walk this way the policeman said
a smile upon his face
just do the time
and pay the fine
next time try not to race.

Walk this way the young man said
and I will show you life
if you will dare
to enter there
I'll make of you a wife.

Walk this way the nurse then said
the birthing room is there
So now's your time
Yes you'll be fine
The baby will come soon

Walk this way, the matron said
just take your time my dear
now here's your room,
you'll settle soon –
we serve with lots of care.

Walk this way the angel said
no more you need to roam
you fought the night
to reach the Light
now enter your heavenly home

Whales

Today a whale played at my front door,
time out from travelling. To join the fun
dolphin acquaintances chase
through choppy seas.

Long fin rises, lazily rolls
and lands on ocean table;
then a tail, large and bifurcated
rears to the Heaven
and falls back to sea
releasing a spindrift wake.
All this at my front door.

And yes an echo of the spume
in miniature, behind,
releasing its own spray
so small that, for a time, I wonder
if imagination has duplicated
my vision.

Together they travel on,
the sea map in their heads
calling them to join the pod
in warmer waters north
or is it cooler waters south?

Does she call her calf as they travel
singing whale songs of encouragement?
Tell stories of far off lands
when he grows weary, or promise fish delights?
These things I wonder
as they pass by my front door.

Behind the Screen

Behind the screen they think
there is no sound.
With strictured breath
in hushed and muted tones
we wait
to hear the beat
of wheel
that shrieks and clatters
its peculiar noise
passing by my ward.
Here,
curtains hide the truth
from knowing eyes,
but cannot drown the sound
of trolleys
lumbering
their slow funeral march
to where the dead men lie.
Upon the bier
the voyage just begun
in passage mute
will travel the cacophony of sounds
to where the silent kingdom can be found.

In here
behind the screens
we breathe again
and know the trolley has passed by
this time,
this ward,
this bed.
But down within that haven of the mute,
alone
the dead man lies,
while here
the screens are swiftly moved away
to wait the passage of another day.

Celebration

I find no cause to celebrate today
for she lies cold and buried in the ground.
No more her smile or laughing voice to share
the moment of the day or week or year.
No more our tears will mingle with the dust,
my ears still listen for the silent phone.
Her Teddy bear sits mutely in my room
his arm outstretched to gently wipe my tears
and Tweety bird will touch my aching heart
reminding me of special bonds we shared.

And yet her voice will echo in my heart –
live life each day – appreciate your friends
and celebrate each moment you can find
in what can seem a harsh and hostile world.

Conflict

Shouts of protest ring through the air.
Faces contorted,
'You're not welcome here.'
You bring with you hatred
bigotry
fear
with your strange way of dressing –
You're not welcome here.'

Angry words, hateful
fly firm and fast
bring hatred
incitement
shades of the past.
Unthinking and careless
we voice our concern –
continue the evil
unwilling to learn.
Indignation spiced with fear
'What will I lose if I let you in here?'

Let There Be Light

Light the candle!

Filled with pain what can be done
but light this single light
within the darkness of the room.

Terror filled,
strike a match.
Flame defiant
licks the edge of darkness
in my soul
sends the shadows fleeing.

Spears of my cocoon
point Heavenward.
A last defiant shriek.

Is this madness of my mind?

Tears across the globe must fall
on nameless images;
cradled in barren arms of agony
safety lies in rubble.

Watch the candle glow
and wake the shadows.
Diminished by
the tiny flame of Hope
they flee
into the darkness
of the night.

www.ingramcontent.com/pod-product-compliance
Lightning Source LLC
Chambersburg PA
CBHW070940080526
44589CB00013B/1584